TANNI GREY-THOMPSON

UNAUTHORISED BIOGRAPHY

John Townsend

Raintree

www.raintreepublishers.co.uk
Visit our website to find out
more information about
Raintree books.

To order:
☎ Phone +44 (0) 1865 888066
🖹 Fax +44 (0) 1865 314091
💻 Visit www.raintreepublishers.co.uk

Editorial: Catherine Veitch
Design: Richard Parker and Q2A Solutions
Illustrations: Oxford Designers and Illustrators
Picture Research: Mica Brancic

Originated by DOT Gradations Ltd
Printed and bound in China by CTPS

ISBN 978 1 4062 0957 0 (hardback)
12 11 10 09 08
10 9 8 7 6 5 4 3 2 1

ISBN 978 1 4062 0965 5 (paperback)
14 13
10 9 8 7 6

British Library Cataloguing in Publication Data
Townsend, John
Tanni Grey-Thompson. – (Sport files)
796.4'2'092
A full catalogue record for this book is available from
the British Library.

Acknowledgements
We would like to thank the following for permission to
reproduce photographs: © Accent Press p. **22**; © Action
Images/Phil Shephard Lewis p. **14**; © Action Press/Rex
Features p. **26**; © Empics Sport/PA Photos p. **23**;
© Getty Images pp. **5** (Phil Cole), **8** (Allsport/Steve
Powell), **11** (Matthew Lewis), **18** (Allsport/Paul
Severn), **20** (Laureus/ Jamie McDonald), **27** (LOCOG/
John Gichigi); © ITV/Rex Features p. **24**;
© Loughborough University/Media Services p. **9**;
PA/TopFoto/Gareth Copley p. **12**; © Photolibrary
Group/Australian Only/Alan Copson p. **7**; © Rex
Features/David Hartley p. **21**; © Times Newspapers/
Rex Features p. **17**; © TopFoto pp. **19** (Jeff Moore),
25 (National News/Wayne Starr).

Cover photograph of Tanni Grey-Thompson in action
in the Paralympic World Cup Athletics reproduced with
permission of ©Getty Images for Visa.

Every effort has been made to contact copyright
holders of material reproduced in this book. Any
omissions will be rectified in subsequent printings if
notice is given to the publishers.

CONTENTS

Some words are printed in bold, **like this.** You can find out what they mean by looking in the glossary.

There are a few very special sports stars who keep winning medals and re-writing the record books. They smash records through hard work, fitness, skill, and constant training. They have a positive **attitude** and a determination to beat the rest. Tanni Grey-Thompson is one of these stars. Her **motto** "Aim high!" inspired her to become one of the great sportswomen in world athletics. As a wheelchair user, Tanni has had to work even harder to achieve her goals.

Tanni's sporting achievements are amazing. She has won 11 gold medals over 16 years at the **Paralympic** Games. She has also won many European medals and London Marathons – and she has smashed more than 30 world records!

The Paralympics

Shortly after the end of World War 2 **veterans** took part in the first sports competition for people with spinal injuries. The event was held at Stoke Mandeville hospital in Buckinghamshire, in 1948. Athletes from the Netherlands joined the competition in 1952, and in 1960, the first truly international competition for people with disabilities took place in Rome, Italy. This was the beginning of what is now called the Paralympic Games, which takes place every four years.

FAST FACT FILE

Name:	Tanni Grey-Thompson
Born:	26 July 1969, Cardiff
Family:	Husband Ian, daughter Carys
School:	St Cyres Comprehensive School, Penarth in Wales
University:	Loughborough University
Famous for:	UK's most successful wheelchair athlete
Major successes	
1988–2004:	Eleven gold medals in Paralympic Games
1992–2003:	Won the London Marathon six times
Honours:	1992 **OBE**, 1999 **MBE**, 2005 Dame Commander of the Order of the British Empire
Charity:	Vice President of "Get Kids Going!"

Today the Paralympic Games involve events for athletes from six different disability groups. In the 2004 Athens Games, nearly 4,000 athletes from 136 countries took part. The Paralympic Games are held in the same year and place as the Olympic Games. London will be hosting the 2012 Paralympic Games and although Tanni Grey-Thompson won't be competing as she has retired, she'll be very much involved in organizing the event.

Tanni won two gold medals at the 2004 Paralympic Games in Athens, Greece.

Tanni was born in Wales in 1969. Tanni's real name was Carys but her sister could only call her "tiny". It sounded like "tanni" and ever since then the name has stuck. Tanni and her sister, Sian, were brought up in the house where their father grew up in Cardiff. Tanni says Sian was a great sister to grow up with..."she's not as competitive as me, but then very few people are! I always knew that I wanted to do sport, and that I had to compete as hard as I could." Although she has lived in many places and travels all around the world, Tanni still sees Cardiff as her home town.

When Tanni was born she had a tiny lump on her back. It didn't seem to bother her and no one knew then that she had a condition called **spina bifida**. Tanni could walk until she was about five years old, but as she got taller and heavier, her legs couldn't support her. She slowly became **paralysed** and from the age of seven, she needed a wheelchair to move around.

WHAT IS SPINA BIFIDA?

The spinal cord is a tube full of nerves that runs through the backbone (the spine). These nerves send messages to and from the brain and around the body. The messages tell muscles how and when to move. "Spina Bifida" means a split or open spine, and it happens when the spinal cord hasn't closed up or grown together properly. This affects the nerves and means that messages don't go to and from the brain as they should.

Tanni believes she was very lucky to be born in Cardiff, the capital city of Wales.

No excuses

Despite having to use a wheelchair, Tanni was determined to make the most of her life and even to take part in games. In fact, she became very keen to win and beat everyone else. She tried a number of different sports, including tennis, basketball, archery, and swimming – but athletics was her favourite and the sport she felt she could do best at. Because her parents taught her to believe in herself and to always try hard, Tanni never gave up playing the sports she loved, and she went on to become an athletics superstar.

"I was one of those kids at school who tried every sport. I had a go at everything. Eventually I found athletics, and I've never looked back." Tanni grew up in a sporty family and often watched her dad play cricket and golf. She was keen to take part too. It was a great way to prove that she was as good as everyone else.

Tanni went to her local school in Penarth, Wales. When she was a teenager, she had to go through a major operation to have a metal rod attached to her spine to straighten it. At this time, Tanni saw something that changed her forever. She watched the London Marathon on television and saw the Welsh athlete Chris Hallam compete in a wheelchair. She was hooked! "I remember saying to my mum that I was going to do the London Marathon one day. It was my dream to be there on the starting line with everyone else. And if you've got that kind of dream it gives you something to aim for."

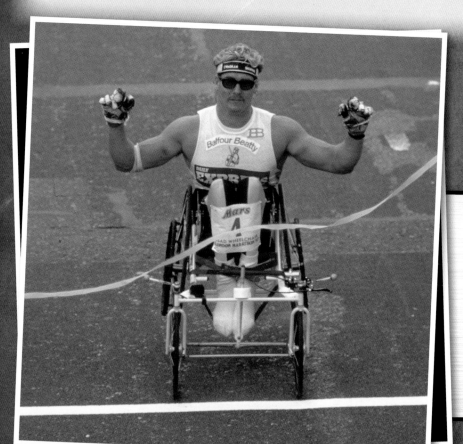

Watching Chris Hallam compete in the London Marathon Men's Wheelchair races inspired Tanni to compete too.

Tanni Grey-Thompson competing at the AAA (Amateur Athletic Association) match on the Loughborough University campus.

Moving on

At first it wasn't easy for Tanni to find somewhere to train in athletics, but she didn't give up. Eventually, she found a sports coach and a club to help her train properly. Just two years after she first tried wheelchair racing, Tanni surprised everyone by winning the 100 metres at the Junior National Wheelchair Games. This was in 1984, when she was 15 years old and competing for Wales. "As I developed as an athlete, I found that I enjoyed writing training programmes and working out what I needed to do."

Tanni went to Loughborough University to study politics, although she was keen to do sport there as well. During this time, there was a date firmly fixed in Tanni's mind. The next **Paralympic** Games were going to be held in 1988 in Seoul, South Korea. Would Tanni be able to compete?

TRAINING HARD

At the age of 18, Tanni became a member of the British Wheelchair Racing Squad and was thrilled to be selected for her first World Wheelchair Games. She made her **Paralympic** Games **debut** in Seoul in 1988 and won a bronze medal in the 400 metre race. It was her big break.

Of all the different races, Tanni prefers the 400-metre distance. "The 400 metres is nice because the start is not quite so crucial and you've got time to get going. I've never been the best starter in the world and however hard I work on my starts, they never really seem to improve that much."

On the road Tanni likes the 10 kilometres because "it's long enough to stretch you, but not too long that you're absolutely exhausted at the end."

Tanni's tips

Tanni often gets asked to give advice to young people who want to get to the top in wheelchair sport. Her answer is to develop both your body and your mind. "It comes back to training – and making sure that it is what you really want to do with your life. If you want to be the best at anything, then it means that you have to make some hard decisions about what you want to do."

STAR TIP

Tanni always keeps a training diary. She writes down things like her heart rate when she gets up in the morning and how she's feeling when she goes out training. She says, "It's a useful record and a good guide to how you are progressing."

Tanni trains hard and warms up carefully for every race, whether it's a road race or an event in the Paralympic Games.

Tough training

Unless you have tried it, you may not think much **stamina** is needed to race along a track in a wheelchair, but you would be wrong. The athlete's arms have to be very strong and wheelchair athletes also need **flexible** shoulders. Tanni was prepared to train hard to build her muscles and upper-body strength. She had to do a lot of warming up and stretching of her shoulders, elbows, and hands. That meant training 50 weeks of the year so that she was always prepared for the next race.

PARALYMPICS

Four years of hard training was all worth it when the next **Paralympic** Games arrived in 1992. Tanni went to the Games in Barcelona and was determined to come home with another medal. In fact, she won four gold medals and one silver, and she broke two world records!

"I went to Barcelona as the world record-holder in four events and I had trained so hard, but you never know until it happens. My family were out there with me and that was great to be able to celebrate with the people who had helped me so much."

Tanni's special racing chair may not be comfortable, but it is fast!

Not only had Tanni proved she was special – but so had her racing chair! It's no ordinary wheelchair; it has three wheels and is about 2 metres (6.5 feet) long. It isn't built for comfort, but for speed. Tanni can only be in her racing chair for two and a half hours before it gets really uncomfortable. When competing at such a high level, it's important to have equipment that fits well. Her chair is made especially for her and she can only fit in it if she's wearing just one layer of **lycra**.

Star of the games

At the Barcelona Games, Tanni became the first woman to complete the 400 metres in less than a minute. This race was exciting to watch and people wanted to see more of the Paralympic Games on the television. Achieving four gold medals at the 1992 Barcelona Games was a big turning point for Tanni. She did well in the next Paralympics in Atlanta too, winning one gold and three silver medals, but it wasn't until the Sydney Games, eight years after Barcelona, that she made major headlines again by winning another four gold medals."Taking part in the Sydney Olympics (in 2000) has got to be the high point of my career. The biggest crowd I competed in front of was 112,000 and it was an amazing atmosphere."

TANNI'S PARALYMPIC MEDALS

Paralympic Games		Medals won
1988	Seoul	Bronze in 400 m
1992	Barcelona	Gold in 100 m, 200 m, 400 m, 800 m; silver in 4 x 100 m relay
1996	Atlanta	Gold in 800 m; silver in 100 m, 200 m, and 400 m
2000	Sydney	Gold in 100 m, 200 m, 400 m, and 800 m
2004	Athens	Gold in 100 m and 400 m

Tanni took part in every London Marathon from 1992 to 2003. She was forced to pull out of the 2006 Marathon due to an elbow injury.

In the same year that Tanni had such great success in Barcelona, she won gold in the London Marathon. Tanni also broke a record in the Lake Sempach Marathon that year – she was the first British woman to finish in under two hours. To have such **stamina** for just over 42 kilometres, and be powered by the upper body alone, is an amazing achievement.

TANNI'S MARATHONS

In her 20-year racing career, Tanni has covered thousands of kilometres. It's exhausting just thinking about the list of marathons in which Tanni has won medals!

1992	London Marathon; Gold Medal, Lake Sempach Marathon; (first British woman in under two hours)
1993	London Marathon; Bronze Medal
1994	London Marathon; Gold Medal
1996	London Marathon; Gold Medal
1997	London Marathon; Silver Medal
1998	Lake Sempach Marathon (personal best time), London Marathon; Gold Medal
1999	Great North Run; Gold Medal, London Marathon; Silver Medal
2000	Lake Sempach Marathon; 6th place (personal best time), London Marathon; Silver Medal
2001	London Marathon; Gold Medal
2002	London Marathon; Gold Medal
2003	London Marathon; Silver Medal

World famous race

The London Marathon has been held each year along the streets of London since 1981. It has become one of the world's top five marathons run over the distance of just under 42 kilometres (26 miles). It is now the largest **annual** fund-raising event in the world, and those who take part raise millions of pounds for charities. Of the thousands of people who race, hundreds are wheelchair users. In fact, the London Marathon is probably the most famous wheelchair race in the country. It's a very hard race and to be allowed to enter it, disabled racers must have completed a full marathon before in under three hours.

Tanni has always been a fighter, sometimes she's had no choice. When she was 11 and looking forward to going to the local high school, a letter arrived telling her that the school couldn't take her because of "her dreadful problems". It was a real fight to get the decision changed. But it made Tanni want to succeed even more.

"There was one thing that I was sure about when I was growing up – I didn't want to be labelled as disabled. I like pushing myself to the limit."

At school, a teacher told Tanni that she should go to college and learn to type, because people in wheelchairs could only work at a desk. "I didn't listen to that – when I told him that I wanted to go to university, he told me that I was probably wasting my time."

Self-belief

Tanni admits that she is very strong-minded. If she decides that she wants to do something, she'll go for it. Her strong character has helped her to deal with painful surgery and comments from others about disabled people. She's put up with being called "a crippled athlete", but the most insulting question she was asked was "Do you have to train?" Tanni smiled and told the truth. "Yes – twice a day, six days a week, 50 weeks a year – about 6,000 hours training a year!"

STAR TIP

Tanni believes in a saying that her grandfather taught her: "Aim high, even if you hit a cabbage!"

This means that you have to have a real goal, do everything you can to reach it – and don't give up if you fail the first time. Tanni hasn't hit a cabbage yet!

Healthy eating

To be a successful athlete, it's important to eat well. Tanni has some helpful rules about healthy eating:

- Eat the right food to train well.
- Eat healthy food most of the time – junk food only sometimes.
- Eat a lot of **carbohydrates** (rice, pasta, potatoes) and a lot of steamed vegetables.

Tanni must train in all weathers to be the best. This can be hard, but Tanni was determined to do everything necessary to reach the top.

All through the 1990s, Tanni continued with her training and racing. Apart from winning medals and trophies, she also began to collect awards that made her even more well-known.

Television awards

Tanni was voted BBC Wales Sports Personality of the Year three times – in 1992, 2000, and 2004. She also won third place at the BBC Sports Personality of the Year in 2000. At this ceremony, there was quite a stir because the organizers forgot to put a ramp for Tanni to get up to the stage to collect the award. But she saw the funny side: "I really felt excited and thrilled, and it was a dream come true. I didn't need to get upset because the BBC are better than that – they had, after all, been at the forefront of showing disabled athletes on the TV."

Tanni, with Olympic rower Steve Redgrave and athlete Denise Lewis, at the 2000 BBC Sports Personality of the Year ceremony.

"It's pretty cool to be Dame Tanni – I never thought this would happen in my life. It shows how far **paralympic** sport has come in this country."

Off to the Palace

Honours are awards given in the United Kingdom for exceptional achievement, service, or bravery. Anyone can recommend a person for an honour. Decisions are made by the Prime Minister and his or her ministers, and passed on to the Queen. A person can be made an **MBE**, an **OBE**, a Dame (women only) or a Knight (men only). In 1992, Tanni received a letter from Buckingham Palace inviting her to collect an MBE. In 2000, the year following her marriage to Ian Thompson, she was presented with an OBE. In 2005, Tanni was invited to the Palace for a third time, when she was named a Dame by the Queen. This was for achievement, sustained commitment, and inspiring the nation.

MOTHER AND DOCTOR

Many people who work find it hard to manage their time and commitments. If someone is also well-known by everyone, it becomes even more difficult to manage public life as well as home life. Tanni had to cope with a busy training programme, a hectic lifestyle, and travelling around the world. Thankfully, her husband, Ian, understood her well – he didn't mind when she went out training on their wedding day!

Tanni says: "It's not easy getting the balance right between being a wife, mother, and athlete. It's tough trying to explain to this little thing, 'This is mummy's job, mummy has to go and train now.' It is really hard because sometimes she just doesn't understand."

Tanni's husband was a **Paralympic** wheelchair athlete himself. Ian was a bicycle racer who was partially confined to a wheelchair after a cycling accident when he was aged 21. Ian became Tanni's coach and took her career very seriously. So much so, that when she told him she was pregnant, he said, "That's fantastic, but you'll be back in training for the Commonwealth Games!"

Tanni gave birth to their first child, Carys, in February 2002. It was a hard time for Tanni being a new mum and having extra training for the London Marathon that was going to take place soon. However, Tanni managed to do both and even won another gold medal.

Changing by degrees

As baby Carys grew, Tanni continued racing, but also began to think about the next stage in her career. The awards kept coming and many of them were from universities that give **honorary degrees** to people considered great **role models**. She has received awards from more than 20 universities to celebrate her own career and also to encourage others to aim high.

Tanni received an Honorary Degree from the school of Health and Social Care at Oxford Brookes University in 2005 for her extraordinary achievements as a disabled athlete.

There are not many athletes who can stay at the top of their sport for a long time. After 10 years of competing at the highest level, many sportsmen and women have moved on. Tanni stayed at the top for 20 years! It was in 2007, at the age of 37, that she decided to retire from racing. She said: "I have always said that I would wake up one day and know that I would not want to do it anymore. There are other things that I want to do and, if I want to be successful, I need to devote more time to those things."

Although Tanni had already written her life story in 2001, called *Seize The Day*, she wrote another short book about herself in 2007. She called this one *Aim High* and it gives plenty of clues about what kept her going for 20 years.

Down the tunnel

Even though Tanni has retired from full-time athletics, it doesn't mean she's stopped supporting or taking part in some of the big events of the year. Having won the Great North Run half-marathon a record eight times, she couldn't resist turning up to hand out water to competitors in 2007. She said, "The water station is on a part of the course I always hated because it's on a hill. I used to pull faces at the volunteers as I went past."

AIM HIGH
TANNI GREY THOMPSON

Tanni's 2007 book was named after her grandfather's saying: "Aim high, even if you hit a cabbage!"

Tanni Grey-Thompson acknowledges the crowd after her final race before her retirement.

In September 2007, Tanni took part in the famous Tunnel 2K event in Newcastle. She raced through the Tyne Tunnel from Wallsend to Jarrow and finished fourth. The race is described as "wheelchair racing at the extreme and definitely not for the faint-hearted." The race is an **adrenaline** rush as racers achieve speeds of nearly 80 kmph (50 mph). Once more, the "retired" Tanni made it all look so easy!

Tanni's campaigning work continues as she launches Carlton's Disability Campaign in 2003.

Success and fame bring responsibility. Many sports stars want to give something to others as a thank you for all they have got out of their sport. Tanni does just that. She knows that, despite all her own hard work, she was given a lot of support to help her achieve her goals. That's why she's been involved with helping others, both in sport and in causes for the disabled. One of the projects she supports is advising a company that makes clothes for disabled children. She belongs to all kinds of organizations to do with promoting sport, which often involves going to a lot of long meetings and public events.

As Vice President of the charity "Get Kids Going!" Tanni works to give disabled young people up to the age of 26 years the opportunity to get into sport. With over 200,000 disabled children and young people in Britain, there's a lot to do to help provide sports wheelchairs and other equipment to enable them to compete in their chosen sport.

A helping hand

Luckily, there's a lot more help available now for wheelchair users than when Tanni was growing up. One of the problems for anyone wanting to get involved in sport is how to find expert help, where to try things out, and how to find out what's going on around the country. That's why Tanni helped to launch Deloitte Parasport in 2007. This is an Internet information service for disabled people to help them find out about local sporting choices and try-out days in different sports around the country. Tanni hopes this sort of help will boost the numbers taking up disability sport in the UK, particularly with the **Paralympic** Games of 2012 racing towards us!

Tanni is a great supporter of the charity John Grooms, *which supports and works with people with disabilities.*

So what does the future hold for Tanni – and are there still challenges ahead? You can bet Tanni has many plans and is still aiming high!

Talking about her plans for the future, Tanni has said, "I am coaching a couple of younger athletes who are working towards the Beijing and London Olympics. I also want to continue with my broadcasting and speaking work, but welcome the opportunity to put something back into sport."

One of Tanni's challenges is to raise her daughter and to beat her husband in a few races! "I may do some marathons in Europe,"she says, "but it will only be for fun. I'll probably still do some road racing for a laugh, and carry on trying to beat my husband! I've beaten him on the road once, but never on the track."

Tanni still wants to campaign for wheelchair users and to educate the public about disability issues. She tells how people stop her in the street and ask all kinds of questions. "If I had a pound for every person who has said, 'What's wrong with you, then?' I would be a rich woman! Another favourite is, 'So, are you confined to your wheelchair, then?' – to which I have replied, 'Yes, I usually sleep in it!'"

Now Tanni has retired from athletics she hopes to spend more time with her husband and daughter.

Tanni joined other sports stars for the launch of the 2012 London Olympics logo in June 2007. A similar symbol will be used for the Paralympic Games.

2008 news

Tanni was involved with the British bid for the 2012 Olympics in London. She's bound to be working hard for the wheelchair athletes training for the 2012 **Paralympic** Games.

Lord Coe, who won two Olympic Golds and broke twelve world records in his career, said of Tanni: "She has dominated her sport for twenty years, she has been an inspiration and has **transcended** disability sport."

Tanni will not just be relaxing from now on: "There is one thing that I know. As one door closes another one opens, and there are plenty of challenges and goals that I still have in my life that will keep me aiming high."

Timeline

1969	Tanni was born on 26 July in Cardiff, Wales.
1980s	Tanni begins race training.
1987	Tanni first represents Great Britain in Track Team.
1988	Tanni wins 400 m bronze medal at Seoul **Paralympic** Games.
1992	Tanni wins 100 m (WR = World Record), 200 m, 400 m (WR), 800 m gold medals, and 4 x 100 m relay silver medal at Barcelona Paralympic Games. Tanni wins her first London Marathon.
1992	Tanni awarded an **MBE**.
1994	Tanni wins 100 m, 200 m, (WR), 400 m (WR), 800 m gold medals, and 10,000 m bronze medal at Berlin World Championships.
1996	Tanni wins 800 m gold medal (WR), 100 m, 200 m, and 400 m silver medals at Atlanta **Paralympics**.
1998	Tanni wins 200 m gold medal, as well as 400 m and 800 m silver medals at Birmingham World Championships.
1999	Tanni marries Ian.
2000	Tanni wins 100 m, 200 m, 400 m, and 800 m gold medals at Sydney Paralympic Games.
2000	Tanni awarded an **OBE**.
2002	Tanni becomes a mother (shortly before winning another gold medal in the London Marathon!).
2003	Tanni wins 100 m, 200 m, 400 m gold medals, and 800 m silver medal at Assen, Holland, European Championships.
2004	Tanni wins 100 m and 400 m gold medals at Athens Paralympic Games.
2005	Tanni becomes a Dame in the New Year Honours List.
2007	Tanni retires from full-time athletics.
2008	Tanni is appointed by UK Athletics to lead a drugs panel looking at drug-taking in British sport.

Amazing facts

Tanni's 16 Paralympic medals, 11 medal placings in the London Marathon and her set of British and world records make her achievements oustanding in the disability sports arena.

Tanni graduated in politics and has well respected views on disability sporting issues, regularly broadcasting on BBC2's *From the Edge* television programme made by and for disabled people.

Tanni's favourite colour is purple. She and her daughter can often be seen wearing matching purple Doc Martin boots!

Tanni is also a well-known broadcaster. She has appeared in many high-profile media programmes, such as *Grandstand*, Radio 4's *Woman's Hour*, and BBC Radio Five Live. She has appeared on many television programmes, including *Celebrity Mastermind*, *Question of Sport*, and *The Weakest Link*.

Tanni had a giraffe named after her at London Zoo (a great honour, as they only name their giraffes after sports stars).

A photograph of Tanni in a wheelchair trying to skip like her friends is really important to Tanni because it shows that no one ever told Tanni that she shouldn't skip, and no one ever told her that she shouldn't try. As she was growing up, her parents never told her there were things she couldn't do, just because she was in a wheelchair.

GLOSSARY

adrenaline hormone produced in the body during times of stress. It makes the body sweat and the heart beat faster.

annual something that takes place each year

attitude how a person thinks and feels about something

carbohydrate mainly sugars and starches. Carbohydrates provide a major energy source in the diet.

debut first public appearance

flexible able to bend and move easily

honorary degree degree that is presented to someone by a university for something they have done in their public life, rather than a qualification achieved through the taking of exams

lycra brand of thin elastic clothing often used in sportswear

MBE Member of the order of the British Empire. It is given to a person in recognition for something that they have achieved.

motto short saying to express a goal or ideal

OBE Order of the officer of the British Empire. It is given to a person in recognition for something that they have achieved.

Paralympics international competitions for athletes with disabilities

paralysed unable to move

patron person chosen as a special supporter of an organization

role model person who is a good example to others

spina bifida serious birth abnormality where the spinal cord is malformed

stamina endurance of energy and strength

transcend to rise above or go beyond the limits

veteran former member of the armed forces during wartime

Books

Aim High (Quick Reads), Tanni Grey-Thompson (Accent Press, 2007)

Modern Olympic Games, Haydn Middleton (Heinemann Library, 2008)

Seize the Day: My Autobiography, Tanni Grey-Thompson (Coronet Books, 2002)

Websites

http://www.disabilitysport.org.uk/
A website all about sports events for wheelchair users and others.

http://www.getkidsgoing.com/
Discover more about the charity Tanni supports, which aims to get disabled children into sport.

http://www.tanni.co.uk/home.html
Find out more about Tanni at her official website.

http://www.tunnel2k.co.uk/
Learn about the famous Tunnel 2K race.

http://www.wheelpower.org.uk/index.cfm
Visit this site to learn all about wheelchair sport.

Disclaimer

All the Internet addresses (URLs) given in this book were valid at the time of going to press. However, due to the dynamic nature of the Internet, some addresses may have changed, or sites may have changed or ceased to exist since publication. While the author and Publishers regret any inconvenience this may cause readers, no responsibility for any such changes can be accepted by either the author or the Publishers. It is recommended that adults supervise children on the Internet.